Baking To Get Baked

By MJ Odingreen (Michael Rubens)

ISBN: 0692705384
ISBN-13: 978-0-692-70538-4

CONTENTS

Acknowledgments

I'd like to thank some people that either directly or indirectly helped with the creation of this cookbook:

Paul Ermisch - my closest friend for going on 32 years. I know I can be a pain in the ass, stubborn, weird, and my humming to myself can make anybody crazy. Thank you for your encouragement, your honesty, and your suggestion that we do this together. I doubt this book would have ever materialized without you. You are everything a best friend is supposed to be.

Susan Ermisch - Paul's wife, and my friend, also of 32 years. Closest thing I've ever had to a sister. Thank you for your help and insight both professionally and personally.

Acknowledgments: Nan, Sherri, Wanda, Karrie, David, Fernando, Sasha, Baker, Drew, Karl, Anika, and all my buds on MassRoots.

Dan Lambert-Thank you for your camera skills and your flexibility around work and family responsibilities. You were also a big hand in the kitchen.

Launie Kettler-You've been a pleasure to work with; you know your stuff. I hope to work with you again on the next book.

And last, but not least: Tomodachi-my compadre, my spiritual guide, my stoner buddy, my wonderful Shiba Inu of the last 13 years. If only you could speak.

Introduction

Regardless of the time of year, there is always a holiday around the corner. And with celebration come gatherings, and when people gather, there's food. So, now you need to provide something, or take a plate to someone else's house... hmmmm, what to bring, what to bring? A three-gallon tub of potato salad from Costco? No. A bottle of wine? Too plebeian. What about baking some cookies, some interesting cookies? Even better, how about baking INFUSED cookies!

Whether you're looking to relax after dealing with a house full of relatives or guests, or trying to stay calm while they're still there, medicated baked goods are a natural option to relieve holiday stress. And if you head out to a friend's house, think how thrilled they'll be if you show up for dinner with a dazzling array of aromatic, homemade edibles that you baked yourself! None of that dispensary bought fare, but delectables that you took the time to prepare yourself. Small gestures can deepen relationships; life isn't about how much money you spend; it's about giving of yourself.

The usual way is not always the best way

The accepted method of making edibles is to infuse butter or oil with cannabis. Vegetable, safflower, coconut, or olive, they all work because THC and other naturally occurring cannabinoids bond with fat very easily. However, I have a number of issues with these methods.

A simpler, quicker method

My method for baking at home with cannabis is quite different than what commercial bakeries in the industry use. Although I have absolutely no scientific research to back me up, I truly believe that my system provides a more fully loaded cannabinoid-rich edible than those made with cannabutter. It's also much faster, less messy, less offensive (stinky), and can be incorporated into any recipe that calls for flour of any type. What is my special method you ask? *'Pot flour'*.

From 2005-2008 I experimented in my tiny second floor kitchen with a number of different kinds of infusions. My initial attempt was making cannabutter - the smell of which made me extremely paranoid that everyone within three blocks knew what I was up to.

I next tried using spent vape weed, which worked well. However, to obtain enough usable material with which to bake, it would have required that I devote most of my waking hours to hitting my Silver Surfer (one of the founders lived 5 minutes away and grew killer buds in his basement).

Then, with a flash of inspiration, I selected 100 of the least nasty roaches, peeled the papers, and removed all the remaining ash. When I was a teenager, we used to make "roach bombs" - joints made entirely of roach weed. Harsher than smoking chili pods, it got us super stoned, and, when there was no weed around, was our savior. As Freewheelin' Franklin used to say, "Weed will get you through times of no money better than money will get you through times of no weed." The edibles I baked in my South Broadway home with roach weed got me ridiculously high, but, of course, tasted like licking the ashtray of a chain smoker.

These experiments with vapor and roach weed led me to the discovery of decarboxylation; yes, my ego led me to believe that I was a fucking weed genius and I had stumbled across a major scientific discovery. I then began using "good" shake to turn into pot flour. There's nothing stopping you from using whole bud to make the flour. However, the cost is going to be two to three times greater than plain shake. "Shake" may not be pretty to look at, but often it is quite potent. When cannabis flower is left in a plastic bag or in a jar, trichomes fall off the flower and gravity takes the little crystals to the bottom of the container. It's these little sparkles that hold most of the psychoactive properties of cannabis. This leftover collection of leaves and crystals is the basis for cannabis flour.

In a typical batch of cookies, I use one ounce of shake. You can use less, but your finished product will be less potent, so you'll have to eat more to get as high.

Before we go any further...

A WARNING: Eating cannabis is by far the MOST POTENT way to consume marijuana. If done with forethought and common sense, the experience can be a tremendous amount of fun, and it can offer significant pain relief. BUT, until you determine your effective dosage, err on the side of caution. Although it's virtually impossible to consume a lethal dose of cannabis, to the novice user, over-medicating with edibles can be an unnerving, extremely negative experience that can potentially scare you off from ever eating infusions again.

The most common reason that people over-medicate with edibles is the delay in the high. When smoked, weed effects begin to take hold within five to 10 minutes; when eaten, cannabis can take as long as two hours before taking hold. I've personally experienced a delay as long as twelve hours. Although there is virtually zero research available, anecdotal evidence shows that the best way to consume edibles is on a very empty stomach, because it leads to a faster uptake into the bloodstream, and therefore, some sense of control over when the high hits you. When eaten on an empty stomach, the effects should begin within thirty to forty-five minutes, and take full effect by ninety. But, remember, everyone's body chemistry is different, and there are many other variables that can potentially affect the onset, intensity, and duration of the high.

The best analogy of over-medicating with edibles that I've been able to come up with is being at an ocean beach and floating out a hundred yards, facing the sand. You know damned well that a huge wave is going to hit you at some point and throw you underwater, but you don't know exactly when the wave is going to molest you, but you know it will.

PLEASE - consume responsibly and share responsibly! These edibles are indistinguishable from traditional cookies and cakes. We do not recommend baking and/or serving these treats if children are or will be present. If you are storing/freezing for later use, please use locking containers.

Decarboxylation: What is it and why is it so important?

In chemistry, the term decarboxylation refers to the removal, or separation of a carbon molecule from another molecule. In cannabis, "decarbing" changes THCA to THC, "activating" the THC to be psychoactive. When you light a bowl or spark a joint, you are in essence, decarbing on the fly. So, the first step in preparing your weed for baking, is to activate it.

Were you just transported to high-school chemistry class? Have your eyes rolled back in your head and is steam already shooting out of your ears? Don't worry, relax your furrowed brow, the rest is easy.

Preparing cannabis flour

All you'll need is a typical 9x13 cookie sheet (also known as a quarter-sheet pan), oven mitts, and a standard $15-20 coffee grinder.

First, make sure you have an oven rack in the center position before you turn the oven on, then preheat your oven to 250 degrees.

Take your ounce of shake and remove any large stems. If you find seeds, you have probably chosen a sub-par bag of shake. Break up any large buds. Spread it out evenly on the cookie sheet.

Carefully place the sheet in the oven and set a timer for 25 minutes. After 25 minutes, remove the sheet pan from the oven taking care to use oven mitts. Turn over all the weed (a spatula works well), and place the sheet back in for an additional 20 minutes. Yes, your kitchen will begin to smell like a grow house, but compared to making cannabutter, the scent is mild.

When the timer dings a second time, remove the sheet of weed and set it out to cool. (Do I need to tell you NOT to set the tray outside where a spring zephyr will scatter your ounce back to nature?) You now have decarboxylated your baking weed. Well done!

Note: Time is based on a significant amount of shake. For smaller amounts, decarbing times are as follows: 1/2 oz to a full oz, 15 minutes initially, then an additional 10. For 2 oz of shake, 20 and 15 minutes. 3-4 oz of shake, 25 and 20 minutes. The cannabis will decarb even more as it bakes in the cookies.

Now it's time to plug in your coffee grinder. Once cooled, scoop a quarter to third of a cup of the decarbed weed into the grinder.

In the pictures, I use a canning funnel to make it easier to transfer the weed between containers. Grind for 15-20 seconds, then pop the top and stir with a plastic utensil. Alternatively, just pick up the grinder with the lid intact and give it a few hard whacks on the bottom with the palm of your hand. Either way, you want to loosen any weed that is sticking to the inside of the grinding chamber. Grind three more times. The goal is to end up with the cannabis particles as close to the size of regular flour particles as possible. Dump the contents into a bowl and continue until the entire ounce is grinded. You now have pot flour! You have completed the first step in becoming an official MJ Odingreen edibles baker!

NOTE: After processing, the pot flour will weigh less than the original ounce (or 28 grams) you started with. For this reason, the recipes refer to using 13 to 26 grams of pot flour.

Using pot flour in these recipes

Equipment needed: a good quality, gram-measuring scale

In all of these recipes, the pot flour replaces an equal amount of flour in the recipe. *This is very easy to do* - here is an example:

- The brownies recipe requires 1 ¼ cups of regular flour and 13 to 26 grams of pot flour.

- Measure (by weight) the desired quantity of pot flour and fill your measuring container.

- Then fill the remaining space with regular flour until your TOTAL quantity of regular and pot flour combined is 1 ¼ cups.

Why not provide a volume measure (by cups) of the pot flour by itself?

When dealing with the finished product - brownies, cupcakes, bars - you'll want to know the approximate quantity of weed in each portion. This is best visualized to most of us in "grams of weed" or more exactly, milligrams of weed. By measuring the pot flour *by weight,* instead of volume, we can more easily estimate the potency of each portion.

Recipes

- Alien Shortbread Cookies
- Nutty Dingleballs
- Banana Nut Muffins
- Fudgy Fingers
- Apple Thumbs
- MJ Odingreen's Classic Brownies
- Stony Scotsmen
- Golden Slumbars

Photo by Christoph Bruan, CC0 1.0 2011

My First Time

The very first time I consumed edibles was in 1980, just a few months after I turned 21. In the summer of that year I traveled to Europe for the first time. I spent my 21st in Saint Ives in Cornwall, drinking Guinness and acting like the classic ugly American. My traveling companion George, and myself, stayed up 'til the wee hours playing our harmonicas, and throwing furniture at one another.

A few months later, after leaving George on Santorini with his adoptive group, the BPP (Beach Peoples Party), I returned to Athens with the thought that I would use my remaining traveler's checks to get myself to a kibbutz in Israel, because I wasn't ready to return to North America. Unfortunately, my plan didn't pan out, and in a fit of frustration, fled Greece and ended up two days later in the train station in Amsterdam. That's when the REAL fun began.

The entire time I was overseas I did not make use of my Youth Hostel Pass until I was in Amsterdam. I chose Fat City, a hostel literally next door to the official clubhouse of the Amsterdam chapter of the Hell's Angels. I ended up in a common room with about eight bunk beds. Having spent my early years in Knoxville, Tennessee, I was immediately drawn to Doug Brown, a Kentucky boy with a slower than molasses drawl, and a "come hang with us" smile. I listened in as a group of Americans talked about finding **Space Cakes**, an edible that had to be experienced to believe. But the best space cakes, as rumor told, were from the legendary, original, Bulldog bar. But they never seemed to have any, so one evening Doug and I made our way across town to the Milky Way, a multimedia center.

We found it, and paid our membership fee of 25 guilders each (about $12.50 American). It truly was a multimedia center, with a tea bar, a liquor bar, an arts and crafts floor, a concert hall, and a full movie theater. We hit the crafts floor first and just as we were told found a table selling Space Cakes. They resembled typical slices of zucchini bread (only with visible swirls of hash oil). They looked so innocent I bought two slices. We wandered over to the liquor bar and bought two cans of Heineken, and found a spot on the floor in the large hallway. As we swallowed the cold brew, we realized that we had nothing in which to smoke our hash. So I carefully dented my Heineken can, whipped out my trusty Swiss Army Knife, and punched tiny holes into the green aluminum, and *voila*, instant hash pipe (a true MacGyver moment.) In between hits, we consumed the space cakes.

At 11:55 we found seats in the movie theater and made ourselves comfortable for a midnight showing of the Marx Brothers movie, *Duck Soup*. About halfway through, I was enjoying Groucho's antics when I suddenly became acutely aware that I was very, very high. I turned to my right to ask Doug if he was as fucked up as I was, but his ear wasn't where I expected it to be; Doug had slid down in his seat, and was staring straight up at the ceiling. No need to ask.

Once the movie was over Doug and I compared notes; we were both convinced that we'd lost control of our bodily functions. So we came up with a solution: all the way back to the hostel, we took turns walking behind the other, confirming no accidents with, "Still dry!"

When we finally reached the hostel, right as we were about to negotiate the stairs, a *perfect* American couple we'd met earlier, came running out from the disco in the basement of the building. Excitedly, they bounded up to us and exclaimed, "Hey Doug! Hey Mike! Come back to the disco with us and dance!" I stared at them with flaming-high eyes and mumbled something completely unintelligible. The look of cherubic excitement drained from their faces and both took two steps back. In his stoned-as-shit Kentucky drawl, Doug managed to say, "Maybe another time." The Barbie and Ken couple turned without a word and sped back to the disco. Doug and I made it up the three flights and flopped on to our respective bunks and fell asleep, only to wake up eight hours later STILL high. As crazy as that evening was, I think it planted the seed for this cookbook, 35 years later.

Alien Shortbread Cookies

Alien from the cannabis-green color they end up being. Inspired by my longest standing friend of 50 years, Nan, who became a master of shortbread baking being married to an Englishman.

Yield: 64

Ingredients:

- 13 grams pot flour
- Unbleached flour, combined with pot flour to make 3 cups total
- ½ teaspoon salt

- ¾ lb. unsalted butter (3 sticks)

- ¾ cup brown sugar

- 1 tablespoon vanilla

Instructions:

- Preheat oven to 350 degrees.

- Combine the flour mixture with salt. Set aside

- Cream together butter and brown sugar.

- Add vanilla to butter and brown sugar mixture. Mix well.

- Add flour into mixture, about ¼ cup at a time, until flour is just incorporated.

- If you are using cookie cutters, chill the dough in the refrigerator for 30 or 40 minutes. After chilling, place dough on floured, flat surface. Using a rolling pin, roll out into ¼-inch thickness. Cut dough into desired shapes, place on a cookie sheet. Bake for 10 to 12 minutes. Remove from oven, let cool on cooling rack, and decorate as desired.

- Alternatively, spread dough evenly in a ¼-sheet pan and bake for 15 to 18 minutes. Remove from the oven and let cool for a few minutes in the pan. While still warm, score the baked dough into desired size (8x8 cuts will yield a recommended 64 pieces).

Abstract Pink Smoke by Cristiana Bardeanu, CC1.0

The Ritual

Recently my mother asked me, "What is it about smoking pot that you like so much?" It's a question I've given thought to before, so I had an answer at the ready. "Aside from the effects, I really enjoy the ceremony of it all.

First, deciding what strain I'm in the mood for, the sound of unscrewing the lid from the jar, selecting the perfect nug and placing it in the grinder; twisting the top back and forth until all resistance is gone, releasing the top and smelling the wonderful terpenes, and carefully tapping out the ground flower on to my rolling tray.

Then pulling out a new Raw organic 1 1/4 paper, rolling the crutch and placing it in the rolling machine (I can't roll a decent doobie by hand any more), filling the plastic pouch with the freshly ground herb and locking the machine closed, inserting the rolling paper and spinning it until it almost disappears, licking the gummed strip with the tip of my tongue and finally, giving it the final spin. Then popping out the finished joint, lightly wetting it between my lips, and lighting it up as I consecrate the ceremony." To which my mother replied, I'm sorry I asked."

Nutty Dingleballs

These tasty balls of fun are a twist on the classic Russian Teacakes. My mom made them for special holidays. I started referring to them as Dingleballs in my early childhood.

Yield: 70-80

Ingredients:

- 1 stick or ¼ lb unsalted butter, softened

- 13 grams pot flour

- Unbleached flour, combined with pot flour to make 1 cup total

- 1 cup toasted pecans (or walnuts or almonds), finely ground
- ½ teaspoon vanilla
- Pinch of salt
- ¼ cup powdered sugar

Instructions:

- Preheat oven to 350 degrees.
- Toast the nuts and grind finely.
- Combine all ingredients in mixing bowl and mix well.
- Chill dough in refrigerator for 60 minutes.
- Roll dough out into 6-gram balls, and place them on an ungreased tray.
- Bake for 15-18 minutes.
- Once they're cooked through, let them cool slightly.
- When they're no longer hot - but still warm to the touch - drop balls in powdered sugar and gently toss until balls are heavily coated.

Kalymnos spongs 1 by kallerno, CC 3.0 2012

Always Be Prepared

So, not long ago I'm finishing up with a customer and I'm about to bag up her single pop-top, and she asks me if the bag is necessary. I tell her if she has an exit bag we can use that, or if she's got something that fastens closed that will work also. She pulls an 8-inch zippered bag from her purse and asks, "Will this work?" She zips it open to reveal 10-12 tampons. "Uh, sure" I say hesitatingly, but so many other responses run through my mind. "Is there a tsunami approaching?" "Too bad we don't have any Flo." "Should I pull out my raft?"

But I kept it together and dropped the container of Sour Diesel in the little bag and zipped it closed. I'm not a prude, but is there no humility left in this world? Geez.

Banana Nut Muffins

These muffins were inspired by a recipe I found in a small Cuisinart cookbook from the early 70's.

For the best portion and dosing size, I recommend using mini cupcake liners and mini cupcake pan (usually 24 cupcakes per pan).

Yield: 36 muffins

Ingredients:

- 1 ½ cups ripe banana, coarsely chopped*
- 13 grams pot flour

- Unbleached flour, combined with pot flour to make 1 ½ cups total

- ¼ teaspoon salt

- 1 teaspoon baking soda

- ¾ teaspoon baking powder

- 2/3 cup brown sugar

- 3 oz. or ¾ stick unsalted butter, softened

- 1 teaspoon lemon juice

- 2 eggs, beaten

- 1 cup toasted walnuts, coarsely chopped

*Bananas are perfect for this recipe when they're ripe, and slightly speckled with brown spots.

Instructions:

- Preheat oven to 350 degrees.

- Puree banana in a food processor until smooth.

- Combine flour mixture, salt, baking soda, and baking powder in a bowl and set aside.

- In a separate bowl, cream the sugar, butter, lemon juice and banana together. Add eggs, and mix lightly.

- Add flour mixture and mix until flour just disappears. Take care not to overbeat.

- Gently fold in the walnuts.

- Place liners in the muffin tin and fill the liners about ½ or ¾ full. Bake for 25 minutes. Check doneness with a toothpick. Remove from oven and let cool.

By Wyeth, N. C. (Newell Convers), 1882-1945 [No restrictions], via Wikimedia Commons

The Newbie

So, I was speaking to my mother recently (87 years old and sharp as a dabbing tool.) She has serious pain in her right shoulder, and she ran out of the CBD oil I brought her on my last visit. I had left a bag of my edibles in her freezer three years ago, but she's been afraid to try them. Well, the pain was so bad yesterday that she couldn't sleep. She was so exhausted that she gave in and ate a piece of one of my brownies.

"It was amazing. Within 10 minutes the pain was cut in half, so I got into bed and slept for 4 hours! I can't remember the last time I slept for four hours! And, your brownies were delicious! It was almost like eating chocolate walnut fudge!"

"Well Mom, it may be my recipe, but you taught me that if you're going to make something, make it the best it can be."

"But something weird happened. Before I fell asleep, I looked at my watch and my watch stopped moving. And when I woke up it was working again."

"Did you forget to wind it?"

"No, it runs on a battery. And, oh yeah, while I was sleeping I had a dream that I went to the fridge to get something to eat, and the handle came off in my hand and I couldn't get anything to eat. I think I had the munchies in my dream!"

"Welcome to my world Mom, welcome."

Fudgy Fingers

This was my absolutely favorite cookie growing up. Ridiculously delicious with a strong cup of coffee.

Yield: 4 dozen

Dough Ingredients:

- 2 1/3 sticks unsalted butter
- 1 ½ cups brown sugar
- 1 tablespoon vanilla
- 13 grams pot flour

- Unbleached flour, combined with pot flour to make 3 cups total
- ¾ teaspoon salt

Filling Ingredients:

- 1 cup toasted walnuts
- 1 ¾ cups semi-sweet chocolate chips
- 1 ½ tablespoon vegetable shortening
- ¼ teaspoon salt
- 1 ½ teaspoons vanilla
- ¾ cup sweetened condensed milk
- 1 ½ tablespoons light corn syrup
- 1 ½ teaspoons water

Instructions:

Dough

- Place softened butter in a mixing bowl and cream together with brown sugar and vanilla. (Take care to fully dissolve the brown sugar.)
- In a separate bowl, combine flour mixture and salt. Using a tabletop mixer, slowly combine butter mixture and flour. (You can also do this by hand, but the mixture is fairly dry and stiff and difficult to move.)

- After combined, remove from bowl, knead by hand for a few minutes to ensure that all the ingredients are incorporated evenly.

- Separate into three equal portions and loosely form into large turd-like shapes about the size of a toilet paper tube. Cover and chill in refrigerator for 1 hour.

Filling

- Adjust the oven rack to the middle position and preheat the oven to 350 degrees.

- Place the walnuts on a cookie sheet and put them in the oven to roast for 2 or 3 minutes. Watch them carefully - they will be done when they just begin to turn brown. Let cool. Chop the nuts into small bits. (Alternatively, place the nuts in a large resealable plastic bag and use a rolling pin or similar heavy tool to break down the nuts into small bits.)

- Melt chocolate and shortening in double boiler and melt completely. Separate a quarter cup and set aside to be reheated later. Let the remaining chocolate cool, off the heat, for 5 minutes.

- Add salt, vanilla and sweetened condensed milk to the chocolate mix. The chocolate will thicken. Mix in the crushed, toasted walnuts.

- Separate the chocolate into three portions, shaped like the dough in previous steps. Refrigerate for 45 minutes.

Assembly

- Take one dough portion out of the refrigerator. Squeeze and form dough into a cylinder 10-inches long. Place onto a lightly floured strip of parchment paper, about 18-inches x 12-inches.

- Roll the dough out into a rectangular shape, 14-inches x 6-inches. You may need to cut excess dough. Reuse this if you need to patch to obtain an optimum shape and thickness.

- Take one fudge portion and form it into a cylinder about 13-inches x 1 1/2 -inches rectangular. Place this rectangle on cookie dough so that it will be centered after the cookie dough is folded over it.

- Fold over cookie dough by lifting the corners of the parchment paper, folding over the cookie, and then carefully peal back the paper to release the dough. Try not to get frustrated, as this step takes practice. Seal the edges. Using a straightedge such as a dinner knife is recommended and makes for a more secure seal.

- Transfer the assembled pastry onto a baking sheet, using the parchment. If not cooking immediately, cover with plastic wrap to prevent drying. The cookie will expand by about ½" during the baking process.

- Bake in oven for 17 to 20 minutes.

- After removing from the oven, let it cool for several minutes. Melt the reserved chocolate, adding the corn syrup and water. Blend well.

- Using the back of a spoon, spread melted chocolate on top of baked cookie.

- After chocolate is no longer shiny, portion the entire pastry with a sharp knife. Approximately ¾-inch cookies are recommended. Wipe the knife between cuts to ensure clean cuts. Cover with plastic wrap and freeze.

Note: If kept in an airtight container, these should stay fresh in the freezer for up to three years.

Sam Hood [Public domain or Public domain], via Wikimedia Commons

Losing My Virginity

My first concert was in 1972. I saw Cheech & Chong in a 3500 seat venue, an old wooden firetrap named The Garden in Vancouver, BC. I didn't even smoke weed yet. I have absolutely no idea why my parents let me go.

As I made my space on the floor directly in front of center stage, about 50 feet back, a long haired hippie-freak (now me), plunked down next to me. He immediately zipped open his backpack and pulled out an old-style, loose tobacco can. With a house key he pried open the top. And what was inside the can of Prince Albert you ask? Not tobacco, but a hundred joints that he began handing out to everyone surrounding us. He offered me one, but I politely refused, being the good kid that I was.

Cheech & Chong were HILARIOUS of course; watching Chong take an imaginary dump onstage as a dog on all fours, while Cheech (also on hands and knees) commented on the beauty and artistry of the imaginary turds was priceless.

Most likely, I received a contact high at the show. But three months later - in a field next to our junior high school - I was sitting in a circle with three of my basketball teammates, smoking my first doobie.

...and the rest, as they say, is history.

Johnny Apple Thumbs

A twist on the classic 'thumb' cookie. I invented these a few years ago.

Note: I highly recommend getting a condiment squeeze bottle to apply the jelly for this recipe. In a pinch, you could use a drinking straw or even a spoon. If using a condiment squeeze bottle, vigorously shake the jelly in the bottle before applying to break up any large chunks and remove air pockets from the mixture.

This recipe creates a small round cookie. It's important to be aware of the amount of cannabis in each cookie when dividing the dough. Based on our results, a 7-gram ball of raw dough will yield 10 to 15 milligrams of THC per baked cookie.

Yield: 90

Ingredients:

- 1 ¼ sticks of unsalted butter
- ½ cup + 1 tablespoon creamy peanut butter
- ¾ cup brown sugar
- 1 teaspoon vanilla
- 2 tablespoons honey
- ¾ teaspoon cinnamon
- 13 grams pot flour
- Unbleached flour, combined with pot flour to make 1 ¼ cups flour total
- ½ teaspoon salt
- 1 teaspoon baking powder
- 1 egg
- Good quality apple jelly
- Turbinado sugar

Instructions:

- Adjust the oven rack to the middle position and preheat the oven to 350 degrees.

- Place softened butter in mixing bowl, and cream it with the peanut butter. Add the brown sugar, honey, vanilla, and cinnamon and combine well.

- In a separate bowl, combine flour mixture, salt and baking powder.

- Using a tabletop mixer, slowly combine butter mixture and flour. You can also do this by hand but the mixture is fairly dry and stiff and difficult to move. After this is fully combined, mix in and fully combine the egg.

- Knead by hand for about a minute, to ensure that all the ingredients are incorporated evenly.

- Cover with plastic wrap and chill for 45 to 60 minutes.

- Remove from the refrigerator and divide the dough into appropriate portions (7-grams is recommended for each cookie). Roll into a ball and place onto ungreased cookie tray about half to three-quarter inches apart.

- Using your finger, create a depression in the middle of the ball about ¼-inch deep. Be careful about the dough cracking - it's not critical but try to avoid it as much as possible.

- Place in the oven and bake for 7 minutes.

- Remove from oven, and using the squeeze bottle, drop a small amount of apple jelly into each depression. Place back into the oven for another 8 minutes.

- Remove and let cool. While still warm, sprinkle with turbinado sugar and serve.

How Sweet It Isn't

Last fall, I was checking in two customers from New Mexico. Both women were excited about shopping in a recreational dispensary for the first time. Both women were in their late 50's, and, not to be unkind, but their looks were fleeting (or fleeing). Both had spent much too much time in the sun without protection, turning their skin to tanned leather. The one pressed up against the reception window had a rather large, flabby chest, much of which struggled to remain constrained behind a tank top at least two sizes too small. Her license said her name was Elizabeth, so I asked her if she went by Liz or Beth. She responded with a smile, "My friends call me Sugar-tits," to which I responded, "Well, I can't put that in your profile, besides, I'm diabetic."

MJ Odingreen's Classic Brownies

A bagel shouldn't be as soft as white bread, just as a brownie shouldn't be chocolate cake. These are dense, fudge-like brownies.

About the walnuts: Brownies with nuts or without. It's an age-old dispute - like which way to hang the toilet paper.

If you're not a brownie-with-nuts person, you can certainly leave them out of this recipe. However, it will change the consistency and volume of the final product. This might result in a stronger high, so consider adjusting the amount of pot flour accordingly. If you include the walnuts, you can also do so without roasting them as the recipe suggests. Make sure to use fresh walnuts, too. If they're in your pantry for awhile, taste them to make sure they haven't turned rancid.

Roasting the walnuts only takes a few minutes, so watch them carefully. When they are ready, they should just begin to turn brown at the edges.

Yield: 128

Ingredients:

- 1 ¼ cup chopped, unsalted walnuts (optional)
- ¾ lb. butter (3 sticks)
- 10 oz. bittersweet chocolate
- 1 ¾ cups brown sugar
- 4 medium eggs
- ¾ teaspoon salt
- 1 tablespoon vanilla
- 26 grams pot flour
- Unbleached flour, combined with pot flour to make 1 ¼ cups flour total

Instructions:

- Adjust the oven rack to the middle position and heat the oven to 350 degrees. Lightly coat 2 quarter-sheet pans with butter.

- Place the walnuts on a cookie sheet and put them in the oven to roast for 2 or 3 minutes. Watch them carefully - they will be done when they just begin to turn brown. Let cool. Chop the nuts into small bits. Alternatively, place the nuts in a large resealable plastic bag and use a rolling pin or similar heavy tool to break down the nuts into small bits.

- Using a double-boiler (you could also use a heat-proof bowl in a pan of water), melt the butter, chocolate and brown sugar until totally dissolved and smooth. Remove from heat and let cool.

- Combine eggs, salt, and vanilla in a large mixing bowl. Add into the melted chocolate, making sure that it is cool enough not to "cook" the eggs. Mix completely.

- Combine flour into melted chocolate mixture a few spoonfuls at a time, only adding more after the previous portion is totally combined. Continue until all flour has been mixed into the chocolate mixture. Add chopped nuts and mix well.

- Divide batter equally between the prepared pans. Smooth and evenly distribute the batter to a consistent thickness. Bake about 16 to 18 minutes. Check doneness using the toothpick method.

  - Let cool for 10 to 15 minutes. Cut the brownies while they are still warm - this will ensure cleaner cuts. Cut each quarter sheet pan in an 8x8 grid. Leave them in the pan until completely cool (putting them in the freezer works well) - they will be much easier to move.

Carefully transfer them to a serving platter or storage container. Refrigerate or freeze any extra portions.

Photo by Richard Lydeker, 1898 (Flickr Creative Commons & American Museum of Natural History Library)

Getting High Is No Bull

Back in January, a couple came in to the dispensary from out of state to inquire about edibles. I began asking my usual questions, "How often do you partake, etc.?" They looked at one another, then back to me, and the man said hesitatingly, "Well, it's not for us...it's for a 1400-pound steer." I stood speechless for a few seconds, thinking that maybe they were just screwing with me. Then, I couldn't stop laughing.

Turns out, the couple was exhibiting the beast (actually a handsome animal, they showed me photos) at the Great Western Stock Show, but he was too jumpy in the ring, and they wanted to calm him down. They had already fed him several containers of peach rings (200 mg), and it helped, but not enough. I sold them two grams of indica oil and suggested starting with half a gram. But I warned them that if they over-medicated the animal, he might just lie down in the ring and go to sleep. And we all know the saying, "Where does a 1400-pound steer sleep? Anywhere he wants."

Stony Scotsmen

When I was about 8 years old, early on Saturday mornings, I'd sit in front of our old black & white RCA and watch cartoons while polishing off an entire bag of butterscotch morsels. This yummy treat is an homage to my Saturday morning ritual.

Yield: 128

Ingredients:

- ¾ lb. unsalted butter (3 sticks)
- 6 oz. + 6 oz. butterscotch morsels, divided

- 2/3 cup brown sugar
- 1 ¼ cups unsalted pecans
- 4 medium eggs
- 1 teaspoon salt
- 1 tablespoon vanilla
- 26 grams pot flour
- Unbleached flour, combined with pot flour to make 1¼ cups total

Instructions:

- Adjust the oven rack to the middle position and heat the oven to 350 degrees.
- Lightly coat 2 quarter-sheet pans with butter.
- Using a double-boiler (you could also use a heat-proof bowl in a pan of water), melt the butter, 6 ounces of butterscotch morsels and brown sugar until totally dissolved and smooth. Remove from heat and let cool.
- Place the pecans on a cookie sheet and put them in the oven to roast for 2 or 3 minutes. Watch them carefully - they will be done when they just begin to turn brown. Let cool. Chop the nuts into small bits. Alternatively, place the nuts in a large resealable plastic bag and use a rolling pin or similar heavy tool to break down the nuts into small bits.
- Combine eggs, salt, and vanilla in a large mixing bowl. Add to the melted butterscotch, making sure that it is cool enough not to "cook" the eggs. Mix completely.

- Combine flour into melted butterscotch mixture a few tablespoons at a time, only adding more after the previous portion is totally combined. Continue until all flour has been mixed into the butterscotch mixture. Add chopped nuts and remaining 6 ounces of butterscotch morsels. Mix well.

- Equally divide the batter between the prepared pan(s). Smooth and evenly distribute the batter to a consistent thickness. Bake about 16 to 18 minutes, or until all 4 corners are light brown. Check doneness using the toothpick method.

- Let cool for 10 to 15 minutes. Cut the butterscotch bars while they are still warm - this will ensure cleaner cuts. Cut each quarter sheet pan in an 8x8 grid. Leave them in the pan until completely cool (putting them in the freezer works well) - they will be much easier to move. Carefully transfer them to a serving platter or storage container. Refrigerate or freeze any extra portions.

Golden Slumbars

I borrowed the name from the Beatles song on Abbey Road. The flavor of white chocolate, toasted macadamia nuts, and browned butter I find irresistible.

Yield: 128 pieces

Ingredients:

- 1 ¼ cups unsalted macadamia nuts
- ¾ lb. butter (3 sticks)
- 6 oz. + 6 oz. white chocolate morsels, divided
- 1 cup brown sugar

- 4 medium eggs
- ¾ teaspoon salt
- 1 tablespoon vanilla
- 26 grams pot flour
- Unbleached flour, combined with pot flour to make 1 ½ cups total

Instructions:

- Adjust the oven rack to the middle position and heat the oven to 350 degrees. Lightly coat 2 quarter-sheet pans with butter.

- Place the macadamia nuts on a cookie sheet and put them in the oven to roast for 2 or 3 minutes. Watch them carefully - they will be done when they just begin to turn brown. Let cool. Chop the nuts into small bits. Alternatively, place the nuts in a large resealable plastic bag and use a rolling pin or similar heavy tool to break down the nuts into small bits.

- Using a double-boiler (you could also use a heat-proof bowl in a pan of water), melt the butter, 6 ounces of white chocolate and brown sugar until totally dissolved and smooth. Remove from heat and let cool.

- Combine eggs, salt, and vanilla in a large mixing bowl. Add the egg mixture into the melted chocolate, making sure that the chocolate mixture is cool enough not to "cook" the eggs. Mix completely.

- Combine flour into melted chocolate mixture a few tablespoons at a time, only adding more after the previous portion is totally combined. Continue until all flour has been mixed into the chocolate mixture. Add chopped nuts and remaining 6 ounces of white chocolate morsels. Mix well.

- Divide batter equally between the prepared pans. Smooth and evenly distribute the batter to a consistent thickness. Bake about 16 to 18 minutes, or until all 4 corners are lightly brown. Check doneness using the toothpick method.

- Let cool for 5 to 10 minutes. Cut the slumbars while they are still warm - this will ensure cleaner cuts. Cut each quarter sheet pan in an 8x8 grid. Leave them in the pan until completely cool (putting them in the freezer works well) - they will be much easier to move. Carefully transfer them to a serving platter or storage container. Refrigerate or freeze any extra portions.

Michael Misses Baking Commercially

Although I especially enjoy tending bud on the recreational side, (and stealing the virtue of so many out of state newbies), I miss the R & D of new infused edibles.

I gain great pleasure in watching the evolution of a new cookie and bringing it to market, not just in getting the flavor dead-on, or the mouth-feel just right, but in nailing down a precise dosage. In Colorado, before a new product can be sold in a dispensary, samples must be tested in an independent laboratory.

I guess I miss standing on a rubber mat, leaning over a stainless work table, gazing at a kitchen full of completely separate ingredients, wondering how I will combine them with weed, to come up with a cookie that fires on all cylinders. Hopefully in the near future, I'll be able to direct everyone to a dispensary that sells my edibles. In the meantime, medicate responsibly my friends.

A Plea from the Author

Folks, all kidding aside, if you have children or teenagers in your home, I implore you to protect them from anything that can do them harm. No matter where you live, whether it is legal, or not, to possess it, it is your responsibility to keep cannabis from falling into their curious hands.

In Washington, Oregon, and especially Colorado, state legislatures continue to pass new laws restricting the packaging and labeling of commercial edibles, but the reality is, no matter how far lawmakers try to make the cannabis industry liable for infused products getting into the hands of people under the age of 21, the true responsibility falls on the adults purchasing these products.

Yes, I'm starting to sound preachy, and you can call me a palavering windbag, but PLEASE, lock up your weed, your pharmaceuticals, your liquor, and especially your firearms.

That said, please enjoy your home made edibles. Have fun, laugh your asses off, and be safe. I will now step down from my soapbox and leave you in peace.

Ever so sincerely,

MJ Odingreen

The 13 Best Strains I've Ever Smoked

I began smoking cannabis in 1972 at the age of 13. Living in a port city (Vancouver, BC), usually assures a wider selection of drugs. As strange as it may sound, I can remember strains, highs and prices from 43 years ago, but I can't recall the names of the couple currently living in the apartment above me.

1974: I'm not sure of the strain, but it was supposedly cured with coca leaves. I recall sitting on a nasty couch with one of my two best friends, Chuck, in an equally nasty three car garage, passing a doobie around with a sketchy guy who went to our school. Chuck and I 'went halfers' on an ounce for $10 each. That's right, a $20 ounce.

We walked up to our junior high school to watch a basketball game. When the ball was dribbled up court, every time the ball was bounced, it echoed 3-4 times. At halftime, my need for an ice cream sandwich overtook my paranoia that I was acting super-stoned. Chuck was babbling something to himself as I crept down the side stairs of the bleachers, slid down the baseline and up the other side of the gym to the concession stand. When I looked up at the cashier, he made eye contact with me and proclaimed, "What the fuck are you on Rubens?" I bought two ice cream sandwiches and somehow made my way back to the bleachers. I have never experienced the same high since.

1976: Grand Forks Gold. Grown outdoors in the Okanagan region of the interior of British Columbia, one of the major fruit producing areas of Canada. I was asked to babysit an eleven-year old juvenile delinquent, the son of the high school shop teacher, and a client in an at-risk young teen program. The family lived just down the street, and as I walked up their driveway, the parents came out in a hurry, thanked me for helping on such short notice, and jumped in their car. As they pulled out, the car stopped suddenly, and the driver window rolled down, "Whatever you do, don't let him drink any beer!" "Okay, I won't let the eleven-year-old drink any beer", I thought to myself.

I let myself in, and found Darryl sitting in the living room watching TV. I introduced myself to the little hell raiser, sat down, and watched the tube with him. After 20-25 minutes, Darryl turns to me and says, "I'm going upstairs to hang out in my room for a bit." "Alright," I respond, "I'll be right here." Twenty minutes later, the kid, still wearing a heavy parka and winter boots, flops down on the other end of the sofa. I swear I smell burned weed, but say nothing. Then, after a few minutes Darryl gets up again, and announces he's going to his room again. He comes down a short time later. Now I'm sure I smell beer. The parade continues two more times, when he sits on the ottoman between me and the TV. Darryl is visibly wobbling from side to side. "Darryl, you're pretty fucked up right now aren't you?" First I see a look of panic, then he breaks into a shit-eating grin, "Yeah," he chuckles. "Wanna' smoke a joint?"

Now, the thought DID occur to me that I shouldn't smoke weed with an eleven-year old child, but let's not forget that I was seventeen, and the kid was already ripped to the gills. I figured what the hell, and smoked a joint with the little derelict. I asked him where he got the weed and he explained that his father traveled up to Grand Forks every summer to help his uncle with his pot crop, and always returned home with two large paper shopping bags full of buds.

I told Darryl he needed to at least pretend to be asleep before his parents came home. He did, and after his parents returned, Dad paid me $40 (at least double the going rate), and asked me if I wanted to smoke a doobie. Being a gentleman, I didn't want to refuse his generosity and accepted. And dad had the real deal. As I made the brief walk across the street and down the cul-de-sac to my parents' house, to this day, I swear the street lights bent down and tapped me on the head as I passed by.

1977: African Sensimilla. The very first time I ever heard the Spanish word for "without seeds." The most beautiful Christmas red and green colors I've ever seen. One pin joint between two people and we couldn't find the car in an otherwise empty parking lot. ($180/oz, by far the most I'd ever paid for a z)

1977: Columbian. Almost black in color. High school graduation weekend...all I recall is running down a hotel hallway in my skivvies, imitating a chimpanzee. ($50/1/4 oz).

...didn't smoke much for about 20 years....

1997: Mystery Weed. My best friends and I laughed so uncontrollably while viewing Ed Wood's *Glen or Glenda* that we couldn't remain in the same room; one of my fondest memories with my friends before life got complicated with kids, divorce, bankruptcies, and other adult bullshit. (Can't recall the price)

2002: DJ Short's Blueberry. My first grow; brought the first generation feminized seeds back from Paradise Seeds of Amsterdam. Extremely narcotic, the high made even better knowing that I created it. ($320 for 10 seeds)

2007: Romulan. The real deal. Perfectly grown, peppery taste, beautiful lime green color. Took my dog for a walk on the High Line Canal...just kept walking...for almost 4 hours. ($90/1/4 oz)

2007: Blue God. Possibly the BEST medicinal strain I've ever smoked. Relieved joint pain, but mostly left me with an incredible sense of well-being...dare I say, left me feeling "groovy." ($300/oz)

2008: Bling. Same black market grower as the Blue God. Exceptional mood enhancer...turned me into a merry prankster ($320/oz)

2008: Sage. Potent with a capital P. Intended to go out into the world and explore, but never left my house ($280/oz).

2010: Cannatonic. The first ultra-high CBD strain I ever smoked, obtained at a dispensary. Weird, numbing high, that ended abruptly after 60 minutes. ($10/g)

2011: LSD. Originating from Barney's of Amsterdam, listed as an indica, but one of the most psychically active, and creativity-inducing strains I've ever inhaled. Grown with love and respect by Duncan at Good Chemistry. ($200/oz)

2014: White Slipper. A sativa dominant cross of Cindy '99 and The White. Knocks down mental barriers and allows free thought and ideas to come bubbling up to consciousness. Terrific for writing. ($180/oz)

That's 13. Allow me to add, since everyone's psyche and body chemistry is so different, it's difficult to say whether every strain that I believe to be fantastic, you will find equally exquisite. But, it's our differences that make the world go 'round. I've had many other memorable strains like SFV OG and Strawberry Cough, but I stand behind my 13. So, what are some of your all-time favorites?

.

ABOUT THE AUTHOR

MJ Odingreen (Michael Rubens) is 56, divorced, has lived in Denver 32 years, the last 13 with his trusted Shiba Inu. He has a BA in psychology, and a minor in creative writing from the University of Denver, 1985.

Awards:

Best New Frozen Concession Item Westword 1998, The Ice Man Cometh Sorbets.

Runner Up Best Edible Longmont Sacred Herbfest 2010, Sweet Cheeba Edibles.

Best In House Edibles Westword 2015,

Colorado Cannabis Company (baker for).

Michael also has over 25 years of experience working in the restaurant and food industry, as well as 7 years in the legal cannabis industry.

Follow Michael on Massroots and Twitter as @mjodingreen.

Made in the USA
San Bernardino, CA
19 March 2017